Gina's Star Collection: Poems

Regina Osiecki

To order additional copies of this book, contact:
Xlibris
844-714-8691
www.Xlibris.com
Orders@Xlibris.com

ISBN: Softcover   979-8-3694-0468-3
               EBook   979-8-3694-0467-6

Library of Congress Control Number: 2023914532

Print information available on the last page

Rev. date: 03/22/2024

A DOG'S LOVELY STRENGTH

A dog with coarse golden fur glowing in the sun
Softness from head petting sends tension on the run
He sometimes referred to by his owners as Bobby-kun
His people are always wanting him to join in on the fun

He's got his other nickname of baggy pants
And of turning cheek when faced with rants
His collar jingles as if letting us know how he feels
While gathering a lot of fellow canine friends at his heels

His golden fur stays attached to us
So as to help us remember how time shared between family is a must
And although he may feel concern regarding his fellows
He tries to keep calm when he lets loose with bellows.

He likes to cast the smells of nature over his faults.
When going about the earth as if in a waltz
But the best thing is the smile that reaches his eyes
Should he find it in himself to be able to ignore his fear's lies

His eyes appear to be decorated with something resembling Kohl
The mighty chest he puffs out to let us know he's alive and has soul
He's got a lightness to him in the form of furry wings
And he has a voice to him that reaffirms his halo rings

In our opinion he possesses the fastest tongue in the east
And loves to flop to the ground after each feast
He's a beautifully gifted dog sent to us by choice
And for that reason, I continue to rejoice.

Because although the sorrow seems tattooed on his face
He continues to drape himself on us with a softness akin to lace
He arches his back like he's a cat curling around the bend
For to replenish his doggy ways his courage is God willing to lend

Out of the goodness of his graces so bushy-tailed and bright-eyed is he
Because he knows he has so much more of his life to see
He loves to provide us with company during each day
So as to help us break away from the fray

And though inside does mud occasionally get brought
He knows of love does he continue to be taught
He uses his tail to warm his nose like it's the latest fashion
And runs outside for a bird of some kind with a dashing

For during these moments does he love to remind
That we are stronger when we combine the good vibes inside
And to be aware that during life we must make things happen
And in these moments of reckoning
We know that it's God's love that comes beckoning

For gallantly galloping does he love to do over a lone fence
Because we know his love of running means his humility is immense
Despite the fact that on him pain tries to leave a curse
He knows that sometimes he must be his own nurse

He has the strength to pull another dog his way
To save them from feeling like they have to enter nonsensical play
Because he enjoys the feeling of his people raring up to go
On his fur do they like to nestle to and thro (i.e., like touching wheat fields)

He asks for permission to be let on the couch by laying his head down
And feeling the love nestling on his head like a crown
On his rear lies something resembling the Venus lady from the picture
Who helps him call out and search for things like it's a creature

He shudders in response to us should he eat an item of food
As well as when he sticks his head in things depending on his mood
In the outside he likes to bury his nose to find a stray bug or two
And acts as an occasional predator to each prey that comes through

He squats in salute of marking his territory as if to say he's happy as can be
But most of all loves to vacation under the shade or the tree

A TYPICAL DAY

Lying in a field of blackened prose
Wishing to sample the smell of a rose
Being pulled up with the help of a friend
So as to direct me to the things I feel I should mend

Makes me feel warmed to the bone
Drinking some hazelnut coffee through a straw
In a more childlike fashion unlike my maw

When having a provision in the more organic sense
It helps you have more focus and be less dense
Henceforth when you now go about your day
Try not to allow the haters to lead you astray

And when we continue to go forth as God's people standing together
We can have a better chance of getting our acts together
Through devotion to being rightly pure in thought and action
One can know then that we should not be called a "distraction" (i.e., value of human life)

In find it necessary during certain moments in life
To loosen the tongue in times of strife (i.e., yoga exercise for the mouth)
Lightness resonating with the earthly quality
To help pay respect to those who may live in poverty

ART JUNKY

Out of thin air
Word follows word
They tie themselves together in knots
But you don't have to linger to understand the double meaning
After neurons fire from one synapse to another you make out two words:
Carpe Diem-seize the day!
So that it doesn't fly away from you
The moments where you first witnessed those words
You find them as your eyes blink away sunlight
Your stomach demands to be filled with verbose ingredients
Feet find floor
As an overstimulated mind imagines flowers growing out of the carpet
The sky is sought but you wonder where the ceiling went
You imagine the picture of a girl half there taking up residence in your room
And in your mind in accordance with the latest book
To get in the mood you investigate Victorian clothing
And run your hands down invisible billowing skirts
Words take shape in your memory
As you gather together a quinoa and cinnamon concoction
You pretend to eat the images and description in the dictionary
To satiate your starving artist side as well as your stomach's gurgling

ASKING TO RECEIVE SERENITY

White hot cold sensation sent to me
What else to do but allow it to be
Then continue acting with a certain flair
Let your ideas bubble through the air

Glistening globe of tiny delight
Resisting sound pollution with all my might
Send it to another child I imagine is in need
But know these objects help make a plant after they seed

Understand with these connecting rhymes
For them I may not win the Noble Prize
Believe in the power surrendering itself to you around each tree
You may not believe you're ready

For the idea of feeling at peace
With your environment
And you never will be
But know you won't always feel down in the dumps about things
God sends you reason to hope by brushing you with angel wings

If he feels you're wrong he and his angels will pinch you to set you straight
And then he shall call upon you in earnest to carry your own weight
As old as the world is know you are younger in some way
Shouldn't this be enough incentive to want to let go of fear today?

FOR THE SPRING

At the alcove in the corner, I sit with my cup
For its colors manifest to fill me up

Wanting to grab the doubt and turn it around
But now I see it's time to stand on both feet

Feel grounded as the earth and my green thumb meet
And allow the beat of the earth's heart to chase away my defeat

I KNOW WHAT YOUR
GAME IS GOD

I know what your game is God
Keeping me guessing just to make me want more
But as I stumble over tongue twisters trying to figure this out
I know I'm more courageous than the words I fling about
I'm like a forty-year-old in a twenty-year-old body
I feel like I've seen a lot and I know enough already
I get into the world of the words
Suddenly I got a lot of questions
And a desire to find out the truth behind them
Now I'm what you call a girl wise beyond her years
You make it seem so easy to get the truth
But even if it's spelled out Why do I want to know more?
Why do I want there to be more?
It seems like there's a certain format to these kinds of things

IF YOU COULD THROW
A GIRL A BONE

Stomach all tied up in knots
As I direct this message towards you
You give me dreams to untangle
And goals to look at from a new angle
As I allow sleep to take me
I feel it's the closest I'll be to you
Until we can meet again
The color I cast on this canvas will imbue
As I discover another wizened storyteller
You can bet that I'll get my thoughts together
But know that patience is not my strong forte
So, to get me to stop you just need to say "Hey"
I want to be known more than the girl at the movies alone
Or the girl who would talk to herself as if holding an invisible phone
I want to be another one God waves into heaven's door
Because of that promise
I don't want to be left alone
I think you'd do me a favor God if you could throw a girl a bone

MEMBRANE FEVER

Arrange by adjacent synapses
Memories of unforgettable relapses
How should I respond to certain stimuli?
With nothing more but a few words to tie
It seems more exciting at first
But then you start to rehearse
What was and what can be learned
A restatement of facts will leave you burned
Rhyming seems to happen without much effort
To put it a different way to make it sound more clever
I may not look at myself with such a perspective
But pertaining to neurons, I prefer subjective
Look at things from other peoples' points of view
The freedom to look outside the box
Looking around at things objective when inspiration knocks
What genius's people have and could be
And they too have never felt freer
What could this mean but super naturalism?
Peering at the world as if through a molded prism
Compared to yesterday I feel like a complete opposite
Trying to hang in there as half an optimist
Morphing from one personality to the next
Although my observable phenomena
Try to follow an emotional test
Loving people despite the lies they may tell
Living a life that seems so fleeting but that's just as well
Obtaining immortality to achieve happiness
Such a thing is not wanted when fiction calls it a creator of madness
Surviving after those you've come to love and trust
Replaying in your mind because you feel that you must
For you see it would be better to apply it to daily life
People's stories should be told even if with darkness they are rife

A separation of one person's personality from another being
Know we got our problems but forever therapy just isn't our thing
A rearrangement of impulses needed to survive
Changing my features into a smile to support my inner drive

PAINTING ON CANVAS

Opera music in the background
It becomes my thought noise
Perhaps I'd prefer it over the boring nature of my thoughts
Perhaps I feel music fits better than word noise
Being marred with an out of place voice
Even reading about it seems wrong
Isn't it more right to imagine people talking
Much like they are instruments singing a song?
As if letters and notes go hand in hand
Though you can't fast forward through this powerful play
Some of people's words will no doubt sink in
And you may feel compelled to hiccup them back out
With your own different take on them
You know this word vomit may not sound or look polite

But to you it means so much more than acting out of spite
Just sharing your own opinion on how the world works
And how you prefer it to work
In your fantasy world of your own creation
There are rules but you hate them
There are rules you must still abide by and you are dissatisfied
With this switcheroo between hate and love
That your mind and body like to do
You ask why can't I act of my own accord
You are told because I don't want you to get too bored
I'll throw these colorful words out there
And paint the world in shimmering images powered by the sun
Of this act I instill because I just exist to have fun
As faulty as my thinking may be
Know it's not always easy to keep them in line
Or have them make sense
It means something different to me
As I look at it a different way each time
Until I rearrange my thoughts again
Based off of something old
To attract more listeners
Wanting to rid my head of overcrowding ideas
Knowing the energy behind it
Which will send it back into me in a multitude of waves
Even in pictures of me that are taken
I want to come to life like that here
But I think I will still have to speak

REACH FOR MY LIGHTHOUSE

God, I ease into the light with you
I search for a way to navigate the gravity and stay true
I wish hard on your mythological followers
So as to not be as much of a pity wallower
Getting along is hard with your web attached to my face
But complain as I do
I cannot get along without performing acts of grace
It's like it remains a full-time job for me
For I feel I can only allow these poems
To show the world who I want to be
I don't have enough courage to tell you otherwise
But I put back in my words a message to throw to the skies
Even in my dreams I feel your surrealistic ways closing over
As if my head is being covered and drowned
Before I could find the four-leaf clover
I feel the suffocating embrace of separation anxiety
Freeing myself from the need
To over accessorize my guilt
Believing each flower that you plant
Will not just gather your warmth only to wilt
How misleading is it to each being when it comes to that?
Isn't loving you supposed to free us from pain and a false heart?
Feeling pulsations vibrate through me as if I have wings inside
Withering around like an attraction from moth to flame
From the heat of my core
Is it because of this that I have life and death to my name?
What is this game you constantly scheme up?
Is your plan to just perpetually say "Raise your holy cup?"
Will the waters of your world eventually recede?

What about those who are in desperate need?
Will there be a destination for all in the light and the dark?
Is Heaven in the clouds on earth or in the stars surrounding earth
I'd rather say that both can leave quite the mark
How come for every motion or way of life
I try to enshroud an eagerness to try new things
Know I'm needed to keep up a sense of sobriety
I become further encased in an even heavier cloud
The more I try to seek out answers the more confused I become
What is it like to have forever as a truth?
Throughout life is it you who helps us remember our youth?
Without your interferences I'd love you even more
I hate the feeling like you're forgetting
Just to make someone's heart flutter and mind soar
In fact, my heart would grow fonder
If you would allow me to find a way to not stray and wander
For each door that you open I fire back stubborn
Because every kiss I'm given is like a sunburn
The feel of you shining upon me shakes me around
You allow me to move when I pick up a new sound
You are one who I enjoy passing on a grin
Because if it's with or without you I know I'll never win

SIMULATION STIMULATION

Drawing forth multitudes of secrets steeped in mystery
Still I ask for the dark stories where one can find a comfort in history
Why continue to suffer when the other option is there
I ponder even as I'm distracted by the smell of pizza embedded in clothes
I put off a fulfillment of things
Tasked with in favor of fighting off unrealistic throes
I create adventure to my liking mentally in the lieu of conversation
The feeling of having my body vibrate
A higher perception of awareness without end
In heaven will there still be issues I need to attend
Though there may be no answers yet
I find I have enough questions to ask

And enough time to kill
When pixelation's come at me from a strange place to my mind
Let the music take you on an upward journey
Try not to falter as you trek where the notes fall from
I'm always searching for something real
Amidst the fleetingness of reality

TECH TEMPO

Because I can speak in computer code
Sometimes I blurt out IOP
Intensively out of plans
Like the next keys on my journey to be patient
Almost like it was on the computer keyboard next to QWERTYU
But even inside your humble abode
Don't you wish it could change?
Waiting it out even if it's thought of as strange
Don't you have a moment to spare?
Don't you have emotional surges to put out there in the air?
Believe in your intrinsic ability
To not leave something for dead
In reference to nouns
Keep them in mind
Even if your fear of the end leaves you overcome with dread
Share your hopes and aspirations with the world
Keep your dwelling free with a working of words
Of life in song
Life exists to help you lift up your hardened hearts
And have the guardians of light stake their claim
To allow you to see through walls
And let yourself go
To pick yourself up after each of those graceful falls
Slumber with the idea that things are going to happen
In your lessons learned from coping
Be glad that despite tough times you have never stopped hoping
Know in facial expressions exists
A wide array of emotions too fast to define
Slowly you figure out the mystery here and there with time

Beneath the matters of discipline
The mind wants to know why one has to lie
Why do we only heal when we gather enough to pry?
Privacy lets itself put up warning signs
But why does reality always attempt to blur the lines
Every time you are on the brink of making a discovery
There's a breaking of many a memory
As if each one is a card put in place
And each one has a different image on its face
You find out some things and you don't feel like it's ever enough
When faced with a diamond in the rough

SENTIMENTAL IN ITS OWN RIGHT

Romanticism dictates speech in thought and manner
I feel information flowing through my being as I clamor
For pen and paper to help my ideas find their way
In my mind's eye I choose from those random colorful pixels all in disarray
I fear the anxiety which comes with uncertainty
I hope some form of them will be a match made in harmony
Reiterating actions of using parts of my brain not often touched upon
Grabbing for the things needed to hold on
What is this creativity I was born with
Why do all these verbs come from seemingly an abyss
Where on earth do these ideas come from?
My efforts to keep them from playing to me
Are much like pounding on a drum

OF THE ECLIPSE

Create your vessel to break out of your shell
Gather the things to which luck has attached itself well
Wrap around yourself the words of wise ones
Trailing from your arms the tendrils of thoughts
That are flowing beautiful like silky ribbons
Make a pathway where there once was dust
As you're doing so be sure to cast away ideas borne of lust
Allow your mind to work to seek out the answer
Let your happiness maneuver around inside you like little dancers
With this addition over your person can you continue to grow?
Imagine as you walk the earth eases back to gather below
Let your senses find the beach where jellyfish
Are lighting up to meet you
And so, by each accident in life
You become marked by more scar tissue

FOEMANCE: JOKER
AND BATMAN

A vigilante with the appearance of a man wearing a bat cowl mask
The other occasionally wearing a straitjacket
After following through with a worrying task
One feels as if the one
Who threw him to the chemicals is one to worship
As if such a bizarre accident gave his life a new purpose
Perhaps he thought he couldn't live a life of good
After such a thing so he turned to the one with the cape and hood
Perhaps he just wanted to make friends
Even with newfound darkness inside
For accidentally did he ingest
Some things that hurt his friendly pride
However, convoluted his actions were
When you look at it in stride
Perhaps he was looking for that special someone
To be the gender reversed groom to his bride
Although perhaps it was only caused by something
That thrives on constant chaotic ill
Maybe it was nothing threatening at all
And he just wanted to live for the moment
For from his inner turmoil did he wish to feel less torment
Here and there maybe did he learn to make light of things
He had the misfortune to find in Pandora's box case
Because he knew he had nothing coming at him of that nature
And wanted to further save others from having to face
Deadly ruin that has plagued men
Throughout various points in time and place
And he wanted others to know
We didn't have to feel like we had to constantly fight
As if caught in a paranoid race
But all that changed when his body was malformed beyond belief
And it shreds him of his humanity
To the point where he turned over a new leaf

FOR MY GRANDPA'S PASSING MAY 2012

You were number one
As warm as the sun
An ace if you will
Who had big shoes to fill
You were never late to eat
Had a smile that wasn't beat
Perfected turkey/falcon terms
Kept glass tables free of germs
You were one of kind
Always quick to help in a bind
Cared for each family member
All which we remember
You were quite a strong bloke
With a collection of many a joke
You were an angel from God
Of whose existence we awed

MIRROR MESSAGES

I don't cry on the outside because of scratchy moods
Because it feels like the cherubs are helping me freely fight
By dancing on hair tubes
Inside it feels like my stomach is being tied in knots
As things come to pass
Feels as if the God's are instilling in me a tough rash
Which earth then lovingly supplies antidotes
For that you can't always buy in cash
If one were to get all beings in aerial view
They'd assume we're growing on top of the land
After which we'd feel
As if Christ has always given us his hand
To help us feel taller despite unknown fears of our own
That we hold inside for each other
Live life for enjoyment of the things your arrow points at
That our Creator has grown
We encompass all sense of emotional directions from him

Things negative and positive come into view
That I didn't have the ability to foresee on a whim
As I continue on my journey
I know it's not all for me
For I know such feelings here come from places too far to see
Despite pain it's amazing how we stay tough
And want to gain a new respect from bad ones
We don't always correlate with well
So, I'll travel softly and still wish strongly for you to cast another spell
It's better to live your best despite thoughts that don't add up
Because from the information you gather from God's loving cup
We know love's messages aren't always clearly audible
As human angels we agree we know our decisions
May not feel completely honorable
But despite that God leaves little to the imagination to let us know he cares
They're up there helping us spread our wings
To help make sure the darkness tears
However weird those cues are they will still build some etching of a path
And we know the sirens will take a form of the ones
Who we wish we could angelically save
If we can only recall how to do the math
And ask to receive a calling from ones beyond the grave

TO GRANDPA IN HEAVEN

(Rest in Peace Grandpa, who died May 9, 2012)

Dear Grandpa
Do you see me still?
From up in heaven being so chill
An angel we call you
And think of you we do
Whether watching Chase Utley perform a winning pitch or hitter
Or Carlos Ruiz crouching to catch one
Making a position of a sitter
Should you get tired of my wishes
Is it you sending me a prick and hoping that it misses?
Do they love you enough up there?'
And is it something you like to show me in the air?
Have you no need for earthly things?
Oh, but don't forget the ones down here
With invisible halo rings
To your level or connection with God I may not see
But I know down here
He also doesn't cast away his children but lets them roam free
With the atoms I am made of
Do the element surely corrode
Do we share them with one another from our separate abode?
Do you know things more now than you did before?
Are all of life's questions answered
When you walk through that final door?
Up there I've heard once that time does not pass much
In the moments separated I have a hunch
That one of my youthful forms I will keep
And I will not fall into a never-ending forever
But above all else I have to wonder
With all the balance between destruction and rebirth
Will this world ever be torn asunder?
Either way I'm willing to continue on in mirth
He's given me no reason not to hope
I've always tried to prevent the tearing down
Of the ability to cope

GRAND POP- A FINE WINE KIND OF GUY

A testament to a grand pop who's aging like fine wine
At the amazing age of eighty-four
His spirit is never poor
You're always welcome at his door
You can crisscross the words on his favorite game
Of the "toilet newspaper"
Much fuss is made to pass the blame
A couple mugs lay smudged
With coffee around the business end
And Pop Pop gets breakfast ready with his famous recipe
While he lends me an eye and wonders
Where my next job is coming from
Then he shares with you
The incredible edible egg's yolk
Into which he mushes his bread
Smearing it all around his mouth
And some in his mustache
It's right up there
Along with the corn of yesterday
For such an old guy he's quite spry
With much wisdom and a keen eye
And a serious love for rye
In the end of bread baking
He has a tendency for picking his teeth
With a sole pinky finger
While before a hearty meal
Does the scent of fish oil tend to linger
And takes time to clear away
The words from his throat
He's one for expressing his opinions
And for dishing out the occasional zingers (jokes)
He feels that staying on one channel is a bore
In fact, that just makes him want to change it more
He has bushy eyebrows he always forgets to pluck
At lakes he feeds bread to a passing duck
And should inside his ears

His earring aid he forgets to tuck
His wife Shirley considers it just her luck
He takes gardening up a notch
While not always bothering to look at his watch
And believes certain problems
Could be fixed with the scotch
Of tape or alcohol
He believes the Church is his second home
Because it makes him like a knight
While under the dome
And he wants to feel
That while we exist hope is free to roam
He likes to add his own successful recipe
Because he feels it's a necessity
To be able to exchange civil pleasantries
He's uniquely honest and down to earth
And still feels inclined to prove his worth
By continuing to claim ownership of his home turf
And shower his family with love ever since birth

GENTLE THOUGHTS

Pieces of threadbare cotton fibers wafting down
Helped me to somehow turn my life around
Like a gentle animal going freely
The world is coming in a lot more clearly
Later however the magic would still exist
Even if it's not how I would normally choose to coexist
There was something to keep my heart from fretting
So as to not forever focus on action regretting
Compassion is shared
Even amongst people who look worn
To remind them that from reality
Their hearts are not torn
For even if your history of scar gathering remains long
Eventually it can burst through you in a spiritual song
To that end we let our angels stay upon our shoulders
Which allows us to be strong on the boulders
Even if a stand cannot be made due to grievances ingrained
Sometimes it's best to not look too phased

JOURNEY INTO
MY MIND'S EYE

Miniature dust clouds captured in sunlight spurts
Not much to it except it hits you where it hurts
The nerves flare up time to time again
With God's love to strengthen us
And help us through each of the things that chain
From this we know how to emphasize
Not just because we hope to go to paradise
But because we love the warmth he created
Even if upon our shoulders we are weighted
We shall not back down
When it comes to spreading peace
And sharing the stories of images of daring feats
At heaven's gate what key might I use
But the one who exists for me
To remember I will never lose
For love extends itself to me
And builds up my gaze
And carries me on a whisper
In the current of life's endless maze
Behind the silence exists a force
Wanting to consume things that bring pleasure
Casting them about my person

So in his eyes I will measure
Being good is just as easy as being bad
A curvature and wringing out
Of a semblance of the spirit I am clad
Trying to use things I have at my disposal
To choose from the verbs expressing his proposal

MAKING A USE OF IT

Hanging onto the new and old
Running into someone that's bold
Picking yourself up once again
Losing one who was once a friend
Dancing in the rain without a care
Catching raindrops in your hair
Taking in scent of flowers near
Helping you put your rear in gear
Looking at the threads people sew,
Helps push away the occasional woe
Feeling the sun's warmth at your face
Keeps you feeling strong throughout the race
Building myself up with a good deed
Allows one to feel less like a weed
So, when I realize that I too need work
I feel less inclined to wear a smirk

THOUGHTS SPORADIC

The Sun does not contain God
It contains promises
Promises of new life being welcomed and abruptly taken
Promises of growth underneath it all
As a result of death
Giving nourishment to all things
Threading through the skin of the rot
Creating what one hopes is a never-ending cycle
Beings are created from nature
Later becoming a part of it
There's comfort in the thought
Of forever being connected to something
But woe to anyone who feels like a prisoner
Raised to the beautiful disaster known as the earth
We strive to feel like the birds
And rise again as it throws obstacles in our paths
We strive to feel God's love for us in our hearts
Jealously bubbles within humans
In contrast to the more easygoing animals
Although we claim to love them and nature
There's a certain extra feeling in the air
One can see it
When a driver dumps out an ashtray despite littering laws
Selfish thoughts occur:
"It will all die anyway; I'm just helping it along."
Health defects appear
But still cigarette goes to mouth relentlessly
If inanimate objects had a personality
They would feel what they surround
A world of half and half
Of indifference and strife
Of peace and concern
Oh gold beaten mortal realm where life dwells
You forever pierce my heart with a knife
With all this where then does the love come from?

Feel the power of the star's presence
It twinkles inside of my soul
My faults are highlighted
I twirl thoughts inside my head forever
Once with the dust

MEMORY FROM A DREAM

During college
Under the shining familiarity of the moon and stars
I lay still after dying
Somehow God still left me with a face to see
As if to seal my current fate
My roommate appears with a shovel in hand
With a wide smile and maniacal glee
She throws it down into the land
Tearing out pieces of me by the roots
I tremble as she kicks around dirt with her boots
It's enough to throw me into consciousness
As I look wildly around the room and see regardless
How she rests across from me as per usual
A surge of energy runs through me then
As if to test this reality and release some frustration
I run to her side and whack her silly with my pillow
As she laughs and shields herself
I feel I did it deliberately
Made it a game
In order to have something to write about

WHAT MADE IT THIS WAY

Should you grab my hand in trust
Expect that the need to go on an adventure we must
Find it within ourselves to believe in each other
For it allows me to find a way to help a sister or brother
Serenading a good deed with the beauty of a smile
Wanting to sit in the sun for a little more while
Absorbing the goodness presenting itself
Storing things of a certain quality in a show of stealth
Should I feel a shimmering on my external being
I'll think again before going ahead and fleeing
A whiteness surrounds me and it echoes purity
It demands a need to stand out from obscurity

MOTHER O' MINE

She chases flies
Like a bat out of hell
She loves to cook clams
On the half shell
She finds the bingo app
Keeps her sane
She feels the kitchen
Is like her domain
She likes to Zumba it up
And keeps coffee in her cup
She devours kevitas like cakes
As well as acai blueberry flakes
At night she likes to mellow
Alerts of dinner with a bellow
She wanted me outside to play
So out of her hair I'd stay
She preps for outings with care
Resulting in a sophisticated air
She enjoys her glasses of wine
And acting with her own design
She is a constant guide in life
And helps if I feel strife

She sets me straight if I roam
And keeps things relaxed at home
We have arguments now and then
One over how I procrastinated again
But despite moments of up and down
I do love to have her around

REITERATE CONNECTIONS

Reverberating words on the edge of my mind
Sending them out to the skies high above mankind
In position to gather butterfly kisses
Another door is helped open
With bodily energy listless
How to grasp hold of astral projection
And hold on the love's protection
Taking in messages of celestial importance
Long foretold ideas of misconstrued happenstance
Acting with a variety of variability
Never stopping to relax
Quickly finding a way to connect and leave new tracks
Leaving a part of myself behind
To help others question mysterious truths
An informant of the invisible muse

PUSHING BACK

Bringing yourself up from a downward trend
Finding you've always had what it takes to start again
Only to know that together
Colors and equality can flourish
Years of rediscovering how to soul nourish
Take a chance on continuing to persevere
Remember it doesn't end for you
Even if you die here
With a song in my heart and questions in my head
I look at the world with a childlike curiosity
And wonder about lives led
Contagious thoughts tightening around me
What will it take to loosen the chains and break free?
Know I can't tell you this personally in honesty
For as a writer I feel it's a way
To regain a sense of solemnity
If I get knocked down I can live on a prayer
I've gotten much stronger under his care

WRITING IT DOWN

Atop the table, where the pens lay
Pick one up from the ashtray
Filling it with ink so dark
Putting it to paper
It hits its mark
Hands maneuvering pen around
Words appear
Slightly profound
Droplets of ink that stain
Lines of darkness to reveal the pain
Rushing sound behind the ear
Stained mud coming here
Dwelling deep inside my mind
Using only words that bind
Piercing indents from the pen appear
Confusion on my mind ebbs near
Clenching the pen tightly in hand
Throwing it hard to land
Among the crumpled ideas thrown out
Pressure rises
I let out a shout
Ink dribbles to the floor
A deep breath
My frustration is no more
Reaching down
I pick up the pen
Ideas soon invade my thoughts again

HUMANE CERTIFIED

Treat your pals with the kindness they deserve
We must convey gentleness and hold it in reserve
For we enjoy healthy thoughts we make readily known
With a clean environment gently being grown
Some blossoms thrive in moonlight
Others heal during the warmth of daylight
Which involves sharing the secrets to a positive well-being
And surrender oneself to one above who is all seeing
Pledge allegiance to keeping calm despite change
Even if these superstitious tactics feel strange
Sometimes you need to face challenges head on
So in new beings darkness doesn't rapidly threaten to spawn
We must feel like
We're symbols of power and confidence
We have the love of many
Building up our conscious
So should we start to feel darkness attack
Be thankful to know
That it is not courage we lack
For we have the ability
To continue to overcome it
So that in Hellfire we don't have to sit
For the sake of the flowers in the valleys
Or peaceful times we must continue to carry
We spread accommodation to those in need
To seek out the helpfulness of God's creed

RESTING EASY

Gathering the earth in shaky hands
Helps retain a calmness about the lands
Because sometimes
When we assume nothing can be done
It's best to look deeper in the dirt
To see what you can make appear
As past wars didn't touch under here
And help make sure that the world
Will again be clear
For when fighting against your pains
You too can feel relief from the devil's chains
Such as when I ride off out of sight
The wheels of my engine are burning bright
As they ride safely through the night
Flowers catch the April showers
Pulsing energy traveling in waves
Reminding me of liking my caves
The niches of animals wanting to be fee
And leaves escaping the feeling
Of being struck to a tree
Sometimes I feel moments
Of wanting to fly away
And not spread too much disarray
Because I love people who spread doves
And then go to rest in their alcoves

SEA GREENS

Detritus of falling teas
Encased below warm seas
Agave nectar spreading lips
Blowing warmth to others with your sips
Feeling the warmth with my hands (gifts)
Taking care to tread lightly across the lands
Calming feelings draping upon your form
Allowing greatness to keep you warm
Beautiful shade shielding you briefly
Carrying you with me most politely
Cradling a lovely smile in my dream
Letting your goodness reign supreme

FEAR FACTORY

Sometimes it would rather think it owns us
Rather than let us think we own it
It may relish the idea of seeing us have a random fit
But realize that you can look back on it and laugh
Let this thing called it know it won't be your last
For you have more days where you will be taken to task
See each journey as a new start
With each hardship let your mind wander a little
As you follow your heart
Know you can help yourself bridge the gap
To allow yourself a well-deserved nap
Believe in the power bestowed upon you everyday
Know in your being heavily does His love weigh
He anchors you to the ground as if it's your last hope
Know from past encounters
Should you consider the desire to be overly anxious
He will tell you "Nope"
Know it's your decision to choose faith over hate
For so happy will he be to see
You did not fall prey to the bait
Peace is amassed from the clouds
They come down to be among the masses
It does what it must to raise our glasses
Know God Hates when his children misbehave
Then he gives them smacks with bad weather
Don't let the evil one shut you out
And disallow you to take care of things better
Don't be discouraged due to each storm
For within it exists a clue
So long as you keep the Jesus which exists
In all in your heart and reach for the stars
You can come to appreciate this place
And just be happy you weren't born on Mars
He stores the familiar inside your heart
And helps you make room for more
He keeps those connections strong for you
With each new show of lore

KEEPING CALM IN THE MIDST OF IT ALL

When you see stars falling
You know love is calling
You should use your body for feeling
(i.e., Pocahontas mentioned: Can you feel the colors of the wind?)
And let Mother Nature do the healing
Try to listen to what I'm saying
But not too much
Because I'll feel like I'm fraying
I'm here to help keep your body warm
And to raise you up above the Storm
To keep your negativity at bay
It's best to follow things day-by-day
By keeping the good times going
And allowing life to keep on flowing

REMEMBER YOU
ARE GOOD

Throughout all of my travels here
Don't be caught by a random jeer
Try to break free from its leer
Even if perception isn't clear
I want you to remember who you are
And to think of yourself as a star
If you should feel in need of love
Be sure to look around and above
Then you'll know that despite your doubt
God would never throw you out
Even if we turn away from things
We can relearn how to see our rings-halos
And if you should feel like your goodness is tossed?
Remember that on the whole you can't be bossed
You can take control of your own destiny
And not assume everything is your enemy
Or dwell in paranoia
Despite everything
I've seen people willing to shadow play
To keep the real monster at bay
And even though fear tends to gather anyway
In the end our angels will forever have their way

AUTUMN LEAVES

Red and greens and yellow too
Swirling to collect in the morning dew
Gathering upon the taste buds
To help continue the work of spuds
Plants with caterpillars resting on their tops
Birds drifting down safely to test in the crops
From the nectar in the leaf
There is much love in the weave
They escape from beautiful lies
Because the soul lies in wait
They know to take to the skies
And what if what we assume was decay
Was actually your fear being pushed away?

A CORNACOPIA
OF HAPPINESS

Flower print on
Outside benches
Painted not unlike
Some wicker fences

A dog that people told to leave
Came upon my hand
And love was felt between

Bugs with gossamer
Wings somersaulting
Along with the breeze
Fluttering amongst themselves

Rising above the cicadas
Casting shadows
Along the minnows
Paper lanterns
Dangling from wires

Paint dripping down fences
Similar to a flower filling up
And casting out its dew
Bumble bees nestle themselves
In each adjacent flower petal
Later helping its neighbor

CREATIVE FLUCTUATION

Band of flowers shimmering and leaving its sanctuary
I want to reach out and touch them
Because it seems to be part of a powerful game we play
Who else but you could send these flashing images
As if destined to be made from your light
I know as painful as waiting is for me
I won't lose the orbs you put into my sight
Listening to the little voices that sound in the crackling air
Believing it to be something made from golden hair
Threads that connect us
Directing themselves toward chakra fields
Binding myself to the idea of the power
That being offered Jesus's blood wields
Then the idea continues that he Offers himself to us
Without fail each day
Images that scare you
He will gladly fix them up for you
And make them okay
It happens so fast
But when these violent images come to past
Know the idea of love
Will allow you to heal up at last
Time was given up for you
So now you must do the same
Be glad to go
And share the second chance in his Name
Know you don't have the choice
To stop downer days
Prophesied from occurring
But for each of these moments
More realization starts unfurling
Know he would never do anything
That he knows would hurt you
Of this he instills in all of us another beginning anew
Of course, tying in this realization could be difficult
And although we all struggle with stress
Listen to the ones that are uniquely imminent
Know hard work is greatly appreciated

And that he doesn't let his stars never hold hands
He wants to keep the old and new
Connected throughout the lands
And although not immediate to your knowledge
We are all free-spirited family
We are intertwined by uncertainty
With feelings of up and down morality
We can be all over the place with our feelings
But if you can put yourself in the shoes
Of those who reconcile by kneeling
You start to believe
That there is better than bad that is offered
And understanding that can take the act
Of a lot of thoughts being bribed and glossed over
Don't be mad because God made you a certain way
According to the rules
We need to forget the idea
That we're merely usable tools
He respects us more than that
And he should be given more credit
He allows us to enjoy the feeling of being free
From blood and darkness
With each ordained merit
Know Jesus lived and died for us
So that throughout our suffering
We could at last feel a measure of consolation
As if when I walk on eggshells
I know I'm not hopeless in my dream fixation
For the ideas of peace
Seems more doable with each day's duration

ACCESS THE MUSE!

Get that inner child to spark a creative thought
Heaven knows its needs can't be bought
Except if you give it a pink thought bubble like cotton candy
By harnessing the machinery called your brain
Allow the buzzing to zoom out
And take the shape of words down the lane
Feel the vibrations pulse through your body
Shiver in delight
As you bridge the gap between another synapse
All jittery on a caffeine high
The best feelings come from the sensation
Of climbing a mountain never to die
Assess all those numbers and words
That shuffle around even in bed
Enjoy all those graphics
Comprising imagery in your head
If you look a little out of it
They might say it's because of your meds
You say that's not true I haven't taken them as of yet

FRUSTRATION

Wandering from one footstep to another
A shaking feeling overtakes me
I get incensed
And a crinkle makes itself known in my forehead
I believe I'm good enough
I can feel that unbridled anger getting worse
A fire in my belly flares greater
Than the electrical firing at each synapse
What words should I stumble upon
So that I don't have another relapse
Could it be that I can ignore it
Until someone reaches out to me in need?
Careening through my brains molecular structure
I try to capture them with kindness
But they escape my mental grasp
The remains of the afterthoughts
Pound against my head
I rub at a fast-forming headache
I try to focus on one thing at a time
But I find all these things
Are of interest to my sponge of a brain
And I forget the headache's existence
In order to focus on this hairsplitting adventure
Multiple sensations ghost over my skin
I put thoughts into them
In the hopes that they become more complex
I still can't help but choke on the word vomit
The words that don't fit
And the ones that don't belong
And I let them crumble away

PERSON IN SHADOW

On the edge of my mind's expanse
You send my heart racing in delight
Reaching for you I try
To navigate through a sea of voices
Dreaming for a sense of coherence
Amidst a longing of an otherworldly life
Something tangible which resembles
The thoughts which pour themselves so openly inside
Desperately stringing words along
Only to watch them fall
And disappear through my outstretched hands
Woe and joy to the ones
Who live with an imaginative soul
They're searching for something fulfilling
While inside this earthly bowl
Awaiting the sharp pang of an incoming thought
I gather them like roses and store them away
The scent disappears but the memory remains
Part of you makes me think of infinity
Another part of me also wants closure
But I suppose one can't have it all
Your shadow now looms over me
Looking up I hold your gaze
You were always in the distance but now you're here
And frantically despite the time spent apart
I look away for something else
I feel a drop in my stomach
Look around and state that I have business elsewhere
But you know better than that
Because you are always guiding me
And I love the realization that you care
Despite my ignorance

SOMETHING LIKE
OUTER SPACE

Fear has me in its grip
I'm falling against time and gravity
Into something kind of like outer space
Intergalactic travel
Without a rocket
Just the wings at my back
They say heaven was a white light
Beyond golden gates
But you have to push through a layer of darkness
To get there
For God only knows how long
I feel my heart rate pulsating
And forcing me down the pathway to my imagination
I'm cut into fragments
And turned inside out into light energy
I see nothing of my original form
Only a bright white light
And I can't fathom how I became like this
My mind felt like someone fumbled with a corkscrew
And upended all memories
I travel like lightning
My synapses are bombarded by so much
I can hardly feel any of it
I feel numb but it's pleasant
So weightless it's no wonder
How I'm able to almost fly
I can't help but question the holes in this experience
Does it end at a long stretch
Of manifesting hovering land
And begin on the other side
I move adjacent to it
But I've got no control over my destination
I float into this white expanse
With my mind having a feeling
Like it contains an electrical storm over water
Bits of past moments of my life are flashing through

Is this a dream because it's not making sense
And I know you can't smell or taste in your dreams
When I have one
I feel like someone's asking me questions
About what kind of dream
That I'd like to have

TWO BROTHERS

Picture of a fellow dog having his back
Smiling at the way he gives his brother a loving whack
Wagging his stump of a tail
With two dogs' butts halved on his right
Having half of his tail cut off
Left more room for his personality to fill up
A blob of paint left on their skin
They lived branded
On a warming and wounded earth
Like the rest of us
Speckled brown with two meaty paws
Set in perfect posture below slobbery jaws
Sharing saliva like they're healing each other's mouths
As would one feel themselves
As an extension of their house
Grass stains galore and paws nearly touching
A little smelly lick for the owners leaving them coughing
Sharing their heart with you
They know they work better in twos

Hair the color of golden wheat puffing out
While watching cat neighbors
Parade themselves around on a leash
Sun marks gently fade into each rolling crease
Zeroing in on that lazy leg cast out to the side
Like a work of art
He doesn't even try to hide
And the rough marks
Like calluses on each elbow joint
From flopping down to the ground
He makes it a point
To showcase it like on a gentleman's coat elbows
One paw climbing over the other
To walk like on a rug
Fur scatters around
As both possess faces much cuter than a pug
One could compare
Their natural beauty to a summer day
And I was hoping
To not write another Shakespeare play

BUNNIES INHERENT

The fluff left my coffee.
Seen from the corner of the eye.
A tumultuousness of drugged steps
On the nature of life
Pitter patter into dreams
Which want to put more around the seams
And fret over not doing it of their own means
As a friend so aptly said
Is it the bunny in me
Needing to hurry and not be still
While still getting nothing done
I think everything is wrong
And put myself in song
Not necessarily into decoration for the room
Which can be both good and bad
Something new always has to happen
Or something old needs to be recycled
To get the attention
Of the system that regurgitates it all
And digests it at hairs breathe.
With feet splayed out like a youth once met
And kept on my camera wall

BREAD BUN

Friendship rang true when my bones rattled
At the sight of dismembered bones of past fellows
Strewn on the road adjacent
As the lines poured one out
For the rain on the windowpane

But when I came back to the hearth
You ran with flavor.
For each different day that turned
Adjacent to each other in the fire
Warmth in your hearts for the gift

It was slow going but the delicacy spread
Of the simple life promised outside my head
With the meat I was promised I could get to next
I had gotten there before but the intro struck

I worried where I'd be if not for this
And collected the fluff loved soulfully
Imprinted every happiness
That left a signature of different kinds

Amongst all this
I grasped the thing that wanted to change
And dragging it in the dirt
The liquid soaked through my earthly cloth

Dust mites had new friends at my swaddled body
The infection rose and left the body
And the swaddled heat expanded outwards
With the very least of my happiness

TICKET EAR

Your ears called for papers
To allow entrance into the room
Feet held the ball
Of the youthful game you foretell

You guarded your secrets under focus point
With no words to accompany
But simple gestures that only we knew
From the earth they would part from

There was a scrounge and a wrinkle on the facet
Of this side of the earth
And the link to my past
You peered at without the ability for tears

It was a horror waiting for something
And you were so curious for it
Blind to the joke we wanted to tell
Because life had figured you out

An incoherency of thoughts follow
And sustenance such as that warrants.
A bigger fool to fill
The space of the mouth of the door

The warmth of the gift you left
To see another gift
Meant for someone here by half
You didn't know that meaning
But we knew it would last
To be something here forever

UNTIL TOMORROW
I'M NOT SURE

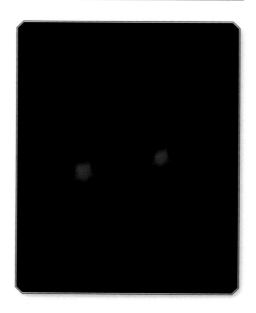

Today the light didn't go up the wall
But the light can even be earned in my gut
And I don't want to talk
About how I would unthread the fibers
Floating amongst the brain fog
My mind feels the pressure of identity
But when I laid on another's hand
Soon after the day I was born on a fringe
I felt my mind splatter paint on itself
A trickle down the pattern of time
Filling in crevices here and there
My body knew its signature best
Long having gotten used to separation
The mind itself a forgone conclusion
I wish I could offer more
But it seems the times I did dried it up
And its so hard to grasp now
Maybe being what it was
The happiness could last
When I contributed
More than white light

OUTSIDE OF
THE FUNGUS

The alcove from another's eye
Reaped me out of the trick
Of fungus caught in tight spaces
Air bubbles tremble me
Over to the hideout I can't leave
Where you never wanted me to stay
Where they lied in their own time
Of a corner in dust
Seconds billow wrinkles on cream fluff
And a creature crawled out of the color
When my mind was at its best
I beheld the object that doubled
When my mind was bored
And not yet made
Until the light of the day hit it

Printed in the United States
by Baker & Taylor Publisher Services